STITCH
AF583780

ISLAND
VIBES

S
A

Weird
but
cute

TO THE BEACH!

Here for the
music

626
I TRIED
WEIRD
626
STITCH
WEIRD
I TRIED
COSMIC

Forever Stitch & Scrump Friends Forever Stitch & Scrump Friends

SWEET YET
SPACEY

SO NOT ORDINARY

Stitch

STITCH & ANGEL
SURF, SAND & SOULMATES

HIT THE WAVES

VIBES

SUMMER

BEACH

HAWAII

SURF CLUB

STITCH
ANGEL

SCRUMP

Very
Persuasive

HELLO UNIVERSE
FAR
OUT